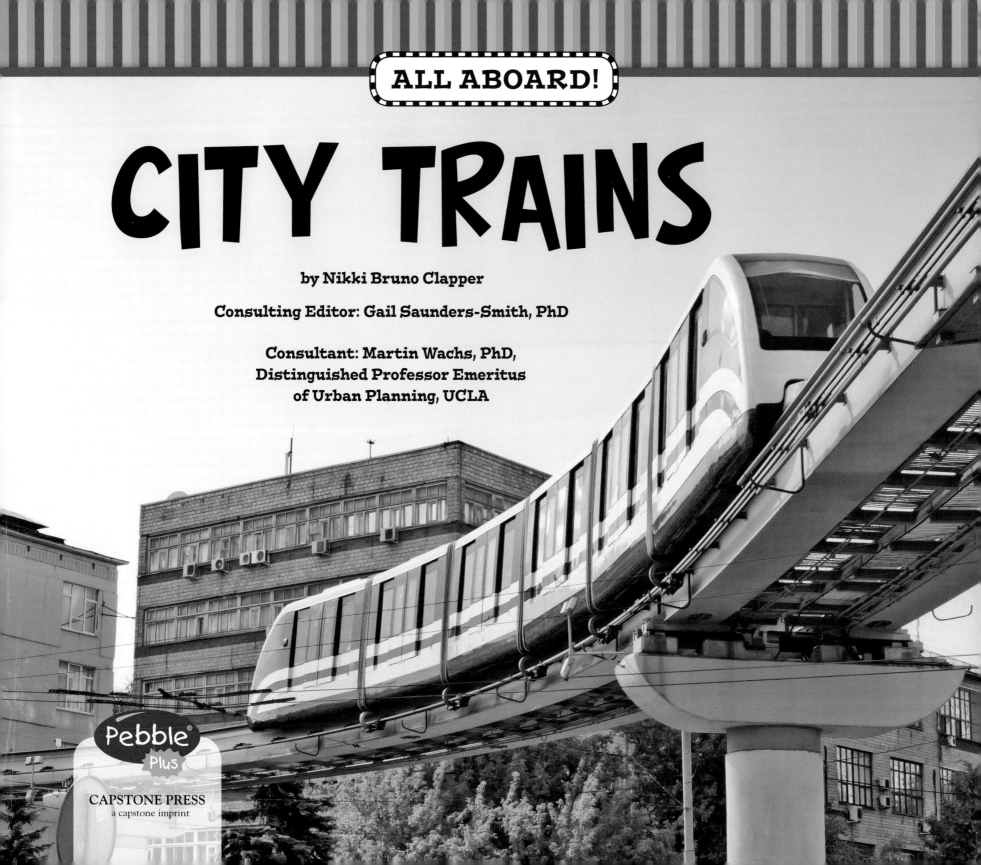

ALL ABOARD!

CITY TRAINS

by Nikki Bruno Clapper

Consulting Editor: Gail Saunders-Smith, PhD

Consultant: Martin Wachs, PhD,
Distinguished Professor Emeritus
of Urban Planning, UCLA

Pebble® Plus

CAPSTONE PRESS
a capstone imprint

Pebble Plus is published by Capstone Press,
1710 Roe Crest Drive, North Mankato, Minnesota 56003
www.capstonepub.com

Library of Congress Cataloging-in-Publication Data
Cataloging-in-publication information is on file with the Library of Congress.
ISBN 978-1-4914-6037-5 (library binding)
ISBN 978-1-4914-6057-3 (eBook PDF)

Editorial Credits
Nikki Bruno Clapper and Linda Staniford, editors; Juliette Peters, designer;
Jo Miller, media researcher; Kathy McColley, production specialist

Photo Credits
Alamy: Agencja Fotograficzna Caro, 11, Chad Ehlers, 9, Directphoto Collection, 7, JLImages, 15, Pegaz, 21, PjrTransport, 19, Rolf Adlercreutz, 5; James P. Rowan, 17; Newscom: Deanpictures/Francis Joseph Dean, 13; Shutterstock: Anton Foltin, cover (train), Denys Prykhodov, cover (phone), oneinchpunch, 2-3, 22-23, PhotoRoman, 1, tovovan, train design element, (throughout)

All the internet addresses (URLs) given in this book were valid at the time of going to press. However, due to the dynamic nature of the internet, some addresses may have changed, or sites may have changed or ceased to exist since publication. While the author and publisher regret any inconvenience this may cause readers, no responsibility for any such changes can be accepted by either the author or the publisher.

Note to Parents and Teachers

The All Aboard! set explores and supports the standard "Science, Technology, and Society," as required by the National Council for Social Studies. This book describes and illustrates city trains. The images support early readers in understanding the text. The repetition of words and phrases helps early readers learn new words. This book also introduces early readers to subject-specific vocabulary words, which are defined in the Glossary section. Early readers may need assistance to read some words and to use the Table of Contents, Glossary, Read More, Internet Sites, and Index sections of the book.

Printed in China by Nordica.
0415/CA21500542
032015 008837NORDF15

Table of Contents

Out of the Darkness

You stand on the
busy platform. A roar
fills the dark tunnel.
Then you see a bright light.
The subway train is coming!

Big cities are crowded.
Trains make life easier.
Many people can ride in
each train car. All aboard!

Away from the Street

Some city trains travel away from road traffic. They ride above or below the street. This saves space and time.

9

City trains are built
for short trips. The cars
have some seats, but most
people need to stand
during rush hour.

Most city trains run on electricity and have human drivers. But some trains have no drivers! They are run by computers.

a subway train with no driver in Copenhagen, Denmark

Spotlight:
The London Underground

The subway in London, England, is nicknamed the Tube. It has tube-shaped tunnels. But only about half of the tracks are underground.

On the Street

Trolleys and trams ride
on tracks on streets.
Busy city traffic can
slow them down.

Trolleys and trams are easy
to use. Passengers don't
have to walk up or down
stairs to get to a station.

Spotlight: San Francisco Cable Cars

The cable cars of San Francisco, California, started running in 1873. Long metal cables pull these railcars up the city's steep hills.

GLOSSARY

cable—a thick wire or rope

electricity—a natural force that can be used to make light and heat or to make machines work

passenger—a person who rides on an airplane, train, or other vehicle

platform—a raised, flat surface; people stand on platforms to wait for trains

rush hour—a time of day when traffic is very heavy, usually when people are going to work or leaving work

train car—one of the wheeled vehicles that are put together to form a train

tram—a public transportation vehicle that moves on a special pathway

trolley—an electric street car that runs on tracks and gets power from an overhead wire

READ MORE

Goodman, Susan E. *Trains!* Step into Reading. New York: Random House, 2012.

Klein, Adria F. *City Train.* Stone Arch Readers. North Mankato, Minn.: Stone Arch Books, 2013.

Peters, Elisa. *Let's Ride the Subway!* Public Transportation. New York: PowerKids Press, 2015.

INTERNET SITES

FactHound offers a safe, fun way to find Internet sites related to this book. All of the sites on FactHound have been researched by our staff.

Here's all you do:

Visit *www.facthound.com*

Type in this code: 9781491460375

 Check out projects, games and lots more at **www.capstonekids.com**

INDEX

Word Count: 181

Grade: 1

Early-Intervention Level: 18